PRAY THE BIBLE

A 10-week Prayer Journey through Ephesians

PRAY THE BIBLE

A 10-week Prayer Journey through Ephesians

by NATASHA WOODCRAFT

Broad Place
publishing
broadplacepublishing.co.uk

First published in Great Britain in 2025

Broad Place Publishing

https://broadplacepublishing.co.uk

email: admin@broadplacepublishing.co.uk

Copyright © Natasha Woodcraft 2025

The author has asserted her right under Section 77 of the Copyright, Designs and Patents Act, 1988, to be identified as the author of the work.

All rights reserved. No portion of the book may be reproduced or transmitted in any form or by any means, electronic or mechanical, including photocopying and recording, or by any information storage and retrieval system, without permission in writing from the publisher.

Scripture quotations are taken from the *Holy Bible*, New Living Translation, copyright ©1996, 2004, 2015 by Tyndale House Foundation. Used by permission of Tyndale House Publishers, Carol Stream, Illinois 60188. All rights reserved.

The views and opinions expressed in this work are those of the author and do not necessarily reflect the views and opinions of the publisher.

A catalogue record for this book is available from the British Library.

Hardback ISBN: 978-1-91503490-8
Paperback ISBN: 978-1-91503494-6

For Jesus, who taught me to pray

HOW TO USE THIS BOOK

For some time, I've been praying Bible-based prayers for friends and family, believers and non-believers. I have found such richness in this practice; such blessing.

Over time, I've adapted the prayers, allowing the words to seep deeper, flow freer and trickle into new places. No two prayers I speak are the same, even if they have the same source. I first had the idea to write these prayers down when preparing a book like this one for a Christian Writers' retreat. I thought others might be blessed by using this practice to pray over their lives and their creative endeavours.

After publishing the prayer book for Christian Writers, I was challenged by a dear friend to extend it to a general audience. And so, *Pray the Bible* was born.

Each day, I share a prayer based on a passage. It's written in poetic form, giving space for your own contemplation and addition. I invite you to consider that passage yourself and write your own prayers or thoughts using the journaling pages. The point isn't for you to spend an extended time *studying* the scripture, though you can if you wish.

The point is to dwell in the words, letting them sink deeply into your soul over a number of days, and inviting the Holy Spirit to enlighten your heart. Then, allow your tongue or pen to flow freely, as you use the Scripture to pray over your life, and the lives of others.

My prayers are simply there to guide. You are welcome to adopt them, but I hope they will be more like a springboard, propelling you to higher heights.

As several of the prayers I regularly use come from Ephesians, the entire text of Ephesians forms the basis of this first prayer book. I believe extra richness and understanding comes from considering verses in their context and I trust that, as you dwell in this book of the Bible for some time, it will become as special to you as it is to me.

The ultimate aim is that *The Word* – Jesus – will speak through *His word* – The Bible – to *your heart*. Then you can speak through His word back to His heart!

There is power in praying Scripture. When we pray Scripture, we can be sure we are praying in the Father's will, and what we ask for will be granted (1 John 5:14-15).

So, how should you use this book?

The short answer is – however you like!

The longer answer is – there is a certain design to it.

Each week considers one section of Scripture as a prayer and breaks it down into five parts – one for each weekday. Each day, one Bible verse is highlighted, but I'd encourage you to read the entire passage for the week every day if you have time. You may wish to pray each small part, or build the whole prayer up over the week – it's entirely up to you. I haven't added the 'Amen' until the end of the week! Then there's the journaling space to add your own prayers, personal thoughts, or anything God speaks to you.

At the end of each week is a *Selah*: an opportunity to pause and listen. You may like to incorporate this in your Friday devotion, or make a special time for it at the weekends, but please resist the urge to skip it altogether. It isn't a catch up page; it's a consolidation page.

There are so many names for God in the Scriptures. Interestingly, 'God' isn't really used as a name like we use it, but as a noun. God is *what* He is, rather than *who* He is.

I don't know what your favourite way of addressing God is, but as I wrote these prayers, I felt led to leave most of the introductions blank. Perhaps you can use your favourite 'My...', or you could try praying with some of the names that Scripture uses? I've listed some here. Maybe think about which name best expresses something from each prayer?

This isn't an exhaustive list. Do add your own in the blank spaces. He is your abba, and He loves to hear your voice!

May the Lord bless you and keep you always,

Natasha x

Names for God:

Father (Abba), Son (Jesus / Yeshua), and Spirit (Ruach)
The Trinitarian Creator (Elohim)
The God who Sees (El Roi)
God Almighty (El Shaddai)
The Everlasting God (El Olam)
The Living God (El Chay)
I AM (Yahweh – The Lord's name)
Yahweh, my Provider (Yahweh Yireh / Jehovah Jireh)
The Lord / My Master (Adonai)
Yahweh, my Healer (Yahweh Rophe)
Yahweh, my Banner (Yahweh Nissi)
The Jealous God (El Kanna)
The Holy One (Qedosh)
Yahweh, my Peace (Yahweh Shalom)

The Lord of Hosts (Yahweh Tsebaoth)
The God Most High (El Elyon)
Yahweh, my Rock (Yahweh Tsuri)
Yahweh, my Shepherd (Yahweh Roi)
Yahweh, my Righteousness (Yahweh Tsidqenu)
Yahweh, who is There (Yahweh Shammah)
God with Us (Immanuel)

Descriptions for God, also used as titles:

The Name (Hashem)
The King
The Husband
The Dwelling Place
The Refuge
The Shield
The Fortress
The Strong Tower
The Judge
The Hope of Israel
The Anointed One (Greek – Christ / Hebrew – Messiah)
The Comforter
Prince of Peace
Salvation (Yeshua - this is Jesus' literal name!)
Wonderful Counsellor

My favourites & My own:

– Week 1 –

Reading: Ephesians 1:1-14

We probably shouldn't have favourite Scriptures, but Paul's astonishing letter to the Ephesians has got to be in my top three, along with Matthew and Isaiah. It is so full of gold that we could mine it for a lifetime and still find something new every day.

Paul lays out God's cosmic purposes in this first section – the ways in which all things were designed to bring glory to Jesus. And the crazy bit? We are part of the plan! Blessed in the heavenly realms, chosen before the creation of the world, chosen to be holy, adopted into His family… the list goes on.

Though absolutely Christ-centric, this passage from Ephesians is also you-centric. Me-centric. It invites us into God's cosmic story.

It doesn't get more astonishing than that!

I hope, as you read Ephesians 1:1-14 daily this week, meditating on the words and praying them back to your God, that this truth will become incredibly real to you.

PRAYER 1

Reading: Ephesians 1:1-14

'Even before he made the world, God loved us and chose us in Christ to be holy and without fault in his eyes.'

Ephesians 1:4

My Abba, my Lord and my God,

Praise be to You – my God,
    The Father of my Lord Jesus Christ.
You are so blessed and so worthy of praise!
May Your father-heart bless me
    with every spiritual blessing in heaven's fountain
    as I dwell in Jesus, my Saviour.
You chose me in Christ,
selected me as Your own before You said,
    'Let there be light.'
You chose me to be holy.

So, make me different,
    set me apart for You.
Oh, purify everything I do
    until it is blameless in Your sight.
I surrender it all –
    from the light of my day to
    the dark of my night.
    All is Yours.

Journaling space

PRAYER 2

Reading: Ephesians 1:1-14

'God decided in advance to adopt us into his own family by bringing us to himself through Jesus Christ.'

Ephesians 1:5

My ....,

I praise You again!
For You lovingly planned for me to be
    adopted as Your own child.
You brought me to yourself –
    somewhere I could never get to by my own effort.
It was Your good pleasure to do this:
    to redeem me and to own me.
Now may all my being
    bring honour to Your name,
May all the work I do, whether paid or unpaid,
    dull or creative,
    flow out of abundant gratitude.
May it bless my fellow sisters and brothers.

For You adopted me into a family – Your family –
    for the praise of Your glorious grace,
    that favour which You so freely clothed me with,
    in and through Your beloved Son, Jesus.
My Jesus, my Saviour.
Thank You for this indescribable gift.

Journaling space

PRAYER 3

Reading: Ephesians 1:1-14

'He is so rich in kindness and grace that he purchased our freedom with the blood of his Son and forgave our sins.'

Ephesians 1:7

My ………………………………………..,

I can never praise You enough.
You are so good!
In Jesus, I have deliverance and salvation
      through His lifeblood which,
         spilt as it was at the cross,
         ran over the altar,
         onto the floor and pooled at my feet.
I kneel in that blood. It washes me clean.
It purifies me,
      providing complete pardon for my sin,
      my rebellion and my wrongdoing.
This is the richness of Your grace
      which You have not just held out tentatively
      but have lavished upon me.

This is how kind You are.
      How much You love me!
I rest in Your grace. I ask You to pour it into my soul,
      filling me to the brim with it,
      that it may overflow into my words, my actions
      and all my life.

Journaling space

PRAYER 4

Reading: Ephesians 1:1-14

'God has now revealed to us his mysterious will regarding Christ —which is to fulfil his own good plan.'

Ephesians 1:9

My ………………………………………..,

Help me to know Jesus better.
Draw me into deeper communion,
    that I may know the mysteries of Your will –
    the wonders You have designed
    according to Your good pleasure.
I know You will bring all things together in Christ.
I can barely imagine what that means, but
    I want to be part of it.
    To be with You in glory.

So I bring everything – I offer it up –
Everything I own that touches heaven and earth
    everything I am that You made in Your image
    everything You've given me to steward.
    All of it.
For my inheritance is Jesus.
    My destiny is with You.
    You have claimed me as Your own.
May all I do, from here-on in,
    be done to make that known.

Journaling space

PRAYER 5

Reading: Ephesians 1:1-14

'And when you believed in Christ, he identified you as his own by giving you the Holy Spirit, whom he promised long ago.'

Ephesians 1:13b

My ....,

I was once far off.
    I wasn't interested in You.
    I belonged to the world.
Then I heard the truth –
    The glorious truth of Your saving grace.
    The wonderful truth of Your sacrifice.
    The incredible truth of Your resurrection power.
    And I believed.
Then You said, *'I'm Yours.'*
So seal me, Holy Spirit.
Be my guarantee –
    the foretaste of my promised possession.
Which is You, Glorious One.
    The triune God.
You are the only possession I want and need.
To my God be the glory
    in everything I do.
May you alone be my inspiration
    and my heart's portion forever. *Amen*

Journaling space

SELAH

At the end of a busy week,

here's your chance to pause.

Be still in God's presence.

Let what you've prayed this week sink into your soul,

and let God speak.

What is He saying to you right now?

Journaling space

– Week 2 –

Reading: Ephesians 1:15-23

As we continue in Ephesians, Paul's attention turns to the church. In this beautiful prayer, he prays that the Ephesian believers might have all the things we're going to pray for: a spirit of wisdom and revelation, the eyes of their hearts enlightened, knowledge of God... It can feel a bit bold to request all these things, but it's scriptural!

Paul is praying this corporately – for our church family are *part* of our inheritance. Have you ever thought of that before?

I hope you have prayer support from your church. If you don't, please ask for it. If you're not yet in a small group with people you trust, please hunt for one. We all need believers in our lives who can encourage, edify and pray for us.

I am a Christian fiction writer, and writing in partnership with the Holy Spirit requires a daily infilling. Every time words flow onto my page, I want them to come from Him. However you give out in Jesus' service, you must remember to feed on the Lord. We were never designed to serve in our own strength. That's why reminding ourselves of the truths about Jesus' majesty in Ephesians 1:15-23 is so important. Those truths fill us up with what we need to pour out.

He is so awesome!

PRAYER 1

Reading: Ephesians 1:15-23

'I pray for you constantly, asking God, the glorious Father of our Lord Jesus Christ, to give you spiritual wisdom and insight so that you might grow in your knowledge of God.'

Ephesians 1:17

Precious Jesus, my Saviour,

Thank You for giving me sisters and brothers
        to join me on my spiritual journey.
Most merciful God,
        Father of my Lord Jesus Christ,
        Grant us, together, deep and intimate insight
        into the true knowledge of Jesus,
        who is *The Way* to You, Abba Father.
Grant to me and my fellow siblings:
        Wisdom that exceeds all earthly wisdom,
        and insight that exceeds that of Solomon.
        Because we know Jesus,
        whom he could only glimpse forward to.

When I open my mouth to speak,
        and open my hands to serve,
May I do so with even greater wisdom than Solomon,
        For I have access to a greater truth
        through Your Holy Spirit in me:
        The Comforter who reveals all things.

Journaling space

PRAYER 2

Reading: Ephesians 1:15-23

'I pray that your hearts will be flooded with light so that you can understand the confident hope he has given to those he called— his holy people who are his rich and glorious inheritance.'

Ephesians 1:18

My ....,

May the eyes of my heart –
    the essential centre of my being –
    be enlightened.
Flood me with Your Holy Spirit,
    blinding me by your grace,
    so I might cherish, with confident expectancy,
    the hope You have called me to.
I have a glorious inheritance in my sisters and brothers.

May I treasure the richness of this calling –
    To dwell with them,
    encouraging, admonishing and building them up,
Seeing no other believer as a rival
    but spurring each on to godliness
    and Spirit-filled living,
    in love.
May we work for Your kingdom together,
    Blessing each other.

Journaling space

PRAYER 3

Reading: Ephesians 1:15-23

'I also pray that you will understand the incredible greatness of God's power for us who believe him. This is the same mighty power that raised Christ from the dead.'

Ephesians 1:19-20a

My ……………………………………….,

I believe You have given me Your Holy Spirit,
Therefore, I have immeasurable,
      unlimited, surpassing greatness within.
The same power that revived Jesus from death
      lives in me!
Help me to believe this,
      to trust Your word,
      to know that You have not given me
      a Spirit of fear
      but of boldness.
You've given it so I might encourage those around me,
      building Your kingdom here.
Your kingdom looks like this:
      Jesus the Messiah magnified.
May Your kingdom come
      and Your will be done
      in all the places where I touch the earth
      just as it is in the heavenly places.

Journaling space

PRAYER 4

Reading: Ephesians 1:15-23

'Now he is far above any ruler or authority or power or leader or anything else—not only in this world but also in the world to come.'

Ephesians 1:21

Yahweh Tsebaoth, Lord of Hosts,

You raised Jesus from the dead! Then –
Seated Him at Your right hand in the heavenly places,
    far above all rule,
        authority,
            power and dominion.
No angels or humans can come close –
    He is above all.
Above every name that can ever be named,
    And every title that men may ever claim.
    Not only in this age,
    but in the one to come.
So I need not fear.
I need not fear speaking the truth. For no earthly kingdoms,
    or pressures,
        or legislation,
            can stand against Your purposes.
All these things will pass away
    but You – Jesus Christ – shall remain.
My God, my Lord, my Deliverer.
The Remainer.

Journaling space

PRAYER 5

Reading: Ephesians 1:15-23

'And the church is his body; it is made full and complete by Christ, who fills all things everywhere with himself.'
Ephesians 1:23

My Jesus,

Everything has already been,
    and will always be,
    put under Your feet.
Jesus, You are head over all and especially,
    over Your body, the church.
So, help me to live well with my sisters and brothers,
    those who are Your body –
    the temples of Your Spirit on this temporary earth.
May our feet be Yours, for Your feet no longer walk here,
    and may our hands serve each other,
    displaying your love to those outside the family.
May love be our defining family feature.

Complete in Your church, and in me,
    all of Your designed works
    according to Your wondrous wisdom and power.
May we be Your temple –
    pure, holy and blameless in Your sight.

Amen

Journaling space

SELAH

At the end of another busy week,

here's your chance to pause.

Be still in God's presence.

Let what you've prayed this week sink into your soul,

and let God speak.

What is He saying to you right now?

Journaling space

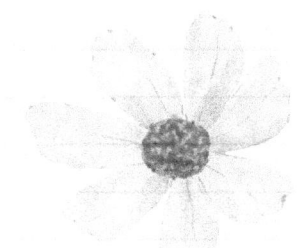

— Week 3 —

Reading: Ephesians 2:1-10

Having laid out God's incredible cosmic plans and cemented us into them, Paul pauses for breath in Ephesians 2. He takes a step back. Why? Because, as we move forward in our calling, hopefully becoming whom He made us to be, it's always important to remember where we came from.

In this passage, Paul walks us through a number of things we once were: dead, disobedient, outsiders, far away… Yet each one is counteracted with the truth of what we have become in Christ, and it's all because of this – God's rich mercy.

The defining moment? We are His workmanship (NIV), or as the NLT so beautifully puts it, God's masterpiece.

Often as we trundle through life, learning from and serving others, we'll feel the weight of our past pulling us down. This prayer gives you a chance to lay that all before the Lord, not hiding it, but claiming His mercy once again. Remember that you are His workmanship. Nothing about you is a mistake.

It's a huge privilege to work for God's kingdom, but it doesn't win us any 'grace points.' No matter how successful we are (or not), we can boast in Christ alone. So, I hope this prayer will protect us from any works-based thinking, keeping us humble before His glorious throne of grace, but secure in the knowledge that *before His throne* is exactly where He wants us to be. No matter what.

PRAYER 1

Reading: Ephesians 2:1-10

'You used to live in sin, just like the rest of the world, obeying the devil—the commander of the powers in the unseen world. He is the spirit at work in the hearts of those who refuse to obey God.'
Ephesians 2:2

Abba Father,

Once I was lost.
I was spiritually dead,
    separated from You.
For I had broken Your law.
My inward rebellion was against You.
I walked in that rebellion,
    happy in it, knowing You not.
I followed the ways of this world,
    influenced by its thinking and catapulted into darkness.
The words of the deceiver seemed good to me –
    those words which questioned You
    and shed doubt on Your goodness.

The deceiver still works.
He still battles against my good intentions
    and pervades the world around me.
I see him everywhere:
    In the disobedient.
    In those fighting against Your purposes.
    In those who live by fleshly passions,

        indulging everything they desire.

That was me once.
Now I know better, yet, I still struggle.
Without the precious conviction of Your Holy Spirit
        I would be captive again
        to every impulse of my sinful mind,
        under the sentence of Your wrath and
        hopeless, like the rest.
So, captivate me, Jesus.
Captivate me, so that I shall never be
        captive to him again.

PRAYER 2

Reading: Ephesians 2:1-10

'God is so rich in mercy, and he loved us so much, that even though we were dead because of our sins, he gave us life...'
Ephesians 2:4-5a

God, my God –
      You are so rich in mercy!
      You have such great and wonderful love!
You loved me with this: The fullness of Your love.
You chased after me
      when I was still in darkness.
You broke through and found me and said,
      'Enough! No more. You are mine.'

Once I was lost.
I was spiritually dead,
      separated from You,
But You made me spiritually alive!
The same life in the resurrected Jesus
      You gave to me, defeating death in me.
By Your grace –
      that unwarranted, unjustifiable merit and favour –
      You saved me from judgement.
You have raised me up
      and seated me with Jesus
      in the heavenly places.
Thank You.

Journaling space

PRAYER 3

Reading: Ephesians 2:1-10

'For he raised us from the dead along with Christ and seated us with him in the heavenly realms because we are united with Christ Jesus.'

Ephesians 2:6

My ....,

I can barely begin to imagine what this means:
    To be raised with Christ Jesus.
My understanding can barely scratch the surface.
As I walk through life,
    it feels so ordinary;
    I don't feel like I am raised with Him.
Yet I know – for You have told me –
    as assuredly as You tell me now,
    that it is done.
    'It is finished.'
    I am raised.
    And it shall be.

So raise me up.
    Raise me up together with Jesus.
      Unite me with my precious Saviour.
      Show me what it means to live
        in the Kingdom of Heaven.

Journaling space

PRAYER 4

Reading: Ephesians 2:1-10

'God saved you by his grace when you believed. And you can't take credit for this; it is a gift from God.'

Ephesians 2:8

My ....,

I am saved by grace!
Show the immeasurable and unsurpassed riches of Your grace
      through the work You do *in me,*
        that all might look on me and see Jesus.
Show the immeasurable and unsurpassed riches of Your grace
      through all the work I do *for You,*
        that all might look on me and see Jesus.

For it is by unmerited favour You have saved me.
    Not by works.
    I cannot boast.
I want to work for You and with You.
I want to work out my salvation with fear and trembling
      and I pray, 'Help me do this.'
Yet protect me from any notion
      that my work achieves Your love.
As my works flourish
      protect me from taking undue credit.
For I am Your workmanship.
    Your work of art.
    Your masterpiece.

Journaling space

PRAYER 5

Reading: Ephesians 2:1-10

'For we are God's masterpiece. He has created us anew in Christ Jesus, so we can do the good things he planned for us long ago.'

Ephesians 2:10

My ....,

I am in awe of that truth:
    I am Your masterpiece,
    first fashioned in Your image,
    then reborn by the Spirit.
For I am created anew in Christ Jesus:
    Spiritually transformed,
    renewed for Your good works
    which You prepared in advance for me to do.
I walk into the good life You have made ready.
Whatever I feel like,
    on my good days and my bad days,
    help me remember that You loved me first,
    and Your love never fails.
Nothing I can do will make You love me more
    and nothing I can do will make You love me less.
Thank You for chasing after me.
Ignite in me a passion to chase after You.

Amen.

Journaling space

SELAH

At the end of another busy week,

here's your chance to pause.

Be still in God's presence.

Let what you've prayed this week sink into your soul,

and let God speak.

What is He saying to you right now?

Journaling space

— Week 4 —

Reading: Ephesians 2:11-22

Once our lives are changed by the gospel, we naturally want to share that – even though we often live in fear!

This prayer puts those desires before our King, asking for the Holy Spirit's help as we partner with Him to illuminate Jesus to the world. I feel like I need to pray this every day, because it is a tough calling and, when we are doing it right, we will often find ourselves under attack.

This prayer also acknowledges, with Paul, that our personal missions are part of a wider mission: to build up the whole body of Christ into a holy temple. We've touched on this theme already, but it will be given more page time here. Whether you work primarily in the Christian or non-Christian sector, whether you serve primarily believers or unbelievers, both can and should be part of this mission of God's: to not just reconcile the individual to himself, but to build a *family* of reconciled individuals.

Perhaps this week, you can consider the way you spend your time. How do each of those activities fit into God's big family plans?

PRAYER 1

Reading: Ephesians 2:11-22

'But now you have been united with Christ Jesus. Once you were far away from God, but now you have been brought near to him through the blood of Christ.'

Ephesians 2:12

My God and my Lord,
    Father of all humanity
        and lover of my soul,

Once I was far off.
I was part of the unchosen,
    with no share in the Messianic promise.
I had no hope.
I knew You not.
Then, in the grace of my precious Jesus,
    You brought me near by the blood of my Messiah.
    The blood that unites all believers in You.

Jesus is my peace:
    The bond of unity
    between me and His church.
He smashed every barrier that separated us –
    all walls of spiritual antagonism –
    that nothing should stand.

Journaling space

PRAYER 2

Reading: Ephesians 2:11-22

'For Christ himself has brought peace to us. He united Jews and Gentiles into one people when, in his own body on the cross, he broke down the wall of hostility that separated us.'

Ephesians 2:14

My............................,
I commit my heart to peace.
In my whole life, help me prioritise reconciliation
     of the one body
     through Jesus' cross,
     putting to death all resentment.
For Jesus abolished
     all hostility caused by the law
          with its commandments
          and ordinances
          and divisions.

He made us into one people group.
     One humanity.
Help me see all earthly divisions for what they are:
     Abolished.
Forgive me for allowing prejudices room.
I commit now to casting them out
     wherever they have taken root.

Journaling space

PRAYER 3

Reading: Ephesians 2:11-22

'He brought this Good News of peace to you Gentiles who were far away from him, and peace to the Jews who were near. Now all of us can come to the Father through the same Holy Spirit because of what Christ has done for us.'

Ephesians 2:17-18

My Jesus,
You preached peace to those far away
    and to those who were near.
Through my works of service –
    through everything You have called me to do –
May I smash barriers,
    showing the way of peace:
Providing for those who are still far off
    to see You,
    to understand,
    and to draw near.
Providing for those who are near
    a new revelation of Your wonder
    through words that You inspire.
It is only through Jesus
    that I can directly approach the Father,
    and only through Your Holy Spirit
    that I can see the truth.
Please reveal any resentment
    that requires my repentance.

Journaling space

PRAYER 4

Reading: Ephesians 2:11-22

'Together, we are his house, built on the foundation of the apostles and the prophets. And the cornerstone is Christ Jesus himself.'

Ephesians 2:20

Holy Spirit, my Comforter,

In my partnership with other believers,
    reveal the Way, the Truth and the Life.
You have created us to be creative.
So in my creativity:
    May strangers be friends,
    Foreigners belong,
    And outsiders dwell within.
For the way is open to all.

Help me live this reality
    through the way I serve others.
Help me build on the foundations
    of the apostles and prophets,
    with Jesus as the chief cornerstone
    of all I do.
Keep me firmly situated on His rock.

Journaling space

PRAYER 5

Reading: Ephesians 2:11-22

'We are carefully joined together in him, becoming a holy temple for the Lord.'

Ephesians 2:21

Jesus, my Messiah,

In You, far off people are united.
    May Your Kingdom increase.
May Your church grow into a holy temple –
    A sanctuary dedicated,
    set apart and sacred
    to the presence of God.
In You, Jesus – and in fellowship with Your family –
    Make me a dwelling place for God the Holy Spirit.
May this be my controlling influence – Your majestic holiness,
    compassion and love.

As I interact with Your church
    make me a vessel of Your voice.
As we interact together
    as Your precious, beloved children –
        make us a dwelling place of Your glory,
        a place of refuge
        and communion with You.

Amen

Journaling space

SELAH

At the end of another busy week,

here's your chance to pause.

Be still in God's presence.

Let what you've prayed this week sink into your soul,

and let God speak.

What is He saying to you right now?

Journaling space

– Week 5 –

Reading: Ephesians 3

Well done. You've made it to Ephesians 3! This is the part you've been waiting for (even if you didn't realise it).

The first half of Ephesians 3 is like a summary of all that's gone before, culminating in the declaration that because of Jesus, 'we can now come boldly and confidently into God's presence' (Eph. 3:12b). Wow!

The second half is Paul's incredible prayer of blessing over the Ephesians, where he commits their spiritual growth to the Father, as he falls to his knees in supplication on their behalf.

Paul longs for the Ephesians to be empowered in the Spirit, to know the incredible hugeness of Jesus' love and to be 'made complete with all the fullness of life and power that comes from God' (Eph.3:19b).

Don't you want that for yourself? I certainly do. And the incredible thing is, because Paul prayed this for the Ephesians, and his prayer made it into our Bibles, we know it's absolutely in line with God's will to pray it for ourselves and for others. Yes, it is OK to pray for this incredible experience of God's love and power to be yours. So be bold – go for it!

PRAYER 1

Reading: Ephesians 3

'...God gave me the special responsibility of extending his grace to you Gentiles.'

Ephesians 3:2b

Abba Father,

Like Paul, You have given me a task.
I feel it in my bones:
    I am meant to live, work, act, create and speak
    for Your glory.
So often I don't feel up to the task.
I know Paul felt that way too:
    insufficient for the task You gave him.
He described himself as the least of the saints.
    Me too!

Yet, You gave him Your unmerited grace
    and commissioned him to preach –
    to proclaim the incomprehensible
    riches of the Messiah.
    To make mysteries plain.
Father, help me proclaim this good news too.
Help me to know, and share,
    the spiritual wealth
    which I don't fully understand,
    but which I know is mine
    in Jesus, my Messiah.

Journaling space

PRAYER 2

Reading: Ephesians 3

'God's purpose in all this was to use the church to display his wisdom in its rich variety to all the unseen rulers and authorities in the heavenly places.'

Ephesians 3:10

My……………………………………..,

Help me to magnify You,
    the God who created all things and all people.
Help me demonstrate the glorious,
    multifaceted
        wisdom of God
            through what I do and say.
Our society so often thinks negatively of Your people,
    and of You.
May my service counter that –
    displaying Your beauty,
    holiness and goodness.
May I walk according to Your eternal purposes.
Your will was carried out through Jesus' incredible sacrifice.
    Once and for all.
He surprised the unseen authorities by
    becoming the Suffering Servant.
Now, may I follow Jesus' example,
    doing as He did.
Not my will, but Yours be done.

Journaling space

PRAYER 3

Reading: Ephesians 3

'I pray that from his glorious, unlimited resources he will empower you with inner strength through his Spirit.'

Ephesians 3:16

My……………………………………..,

Give me boldness to approach Your throne of grace
    freely and courageously,
        through faith in Jesus.
He has done it all,
    paving the pathway with his blood.
    Nothing can remove it.
For this reason, I approach.
    I bow my knees, Abba.
You are the Creator.
Without You, nothing would exist.
    Not me, nor my friends,
    nor my enemies.
You know all the hairs on every head.

Strengthen me from the riches of Your glory,
Energise me with Your power through the Holy Spirit.
Holy Spirit, reach into my inner self,
    all my being and personality,
    and plant Yourself there.

Journaling space

PRAYER 4

Reading: Ephesians 3

'Then Christ will make his home in your hearts as you trust in him. Your roots will grow down into God's love and keep you strong.'

Ephesians 3:17

Jesus, may You dwell in my heart
    so tangibly that I know You are there
    every minute and every hour.
    Make your home in me.
Root me in Your love.
    Ground me like the deep, deep roots
    of the tallest tree –
    like a Cedar of Lebanon
    or a Californian Redwood.
Help me comprehend with all God's people:
    the highest heights,
        the deepest depths,
            the longest lengths
                and the widest widths
    of Your unconditional, agapé love.
If any doubt exists in my heart,
    telling me You don't love me,
    cast it to the wind!
Then counter it with a full experience of
    Your amazing,
    endless adoration.

Yours is the love of the prodigal God
    who ran after me,
    threw His robe around me,
    disregarding all I had done against Him.
May I come to know through personal experience –
    not just information –
    the love of Jesus, my Messiah,
    which far surpasses mere knowledge.

PRAYER 5

Reading: Ephesians 3

'Then you will be made complete with all the fullness of life and power that comes from God.'

Ephesians 3:19b

My............................,
Fill me with all Your fullness,
    the richest experience of Your presence in my life,
    flooding my self with Yourself.
Oh God, Creator of the heavens and the earth,
    who stooped to redeem a tiny, beloved one – me!
You are able to carry out Your purposes.
You are able to do superabundantly more
    than all I could dare ask
    or even think:
Infinitely more than my greatest prayers,
    Extravagantly more than my hopes,
    Lavishly more than my dreams.
You can do this according to Your power
    at work in me.
To You – Heavenly Father,
    Magnificent Creator,
    Perfect Redeemer, Lover of my soul –
  To You be the glory in me,
    in Your church,
    and in Jesus, my Messiah,
    throughout all generations,
    forever and ever. *Amen*

Journaling space

SELAH

At the end of another busy week,

here's your chance to pause.

Be still in God's presence.

Let what you've prayed this week sink into your soul,

and let God speak.

What is He saying to you right now?

Journaling space

— Week 6 —

Reading: Ephesians 4:1-16

You'll have gathered by now that we are not alone. God never calls us to do something then leaves us to it. Ephesians 4 explores this idea more, so we're going to pray it through together.

Within this week, allow yourself space to consider the different tasks that God has called you to. Do you know what they are? Have you had a specific calling, or are you doing some things just because you've always done them (or you've been asked to and haven't known how to refuse?) Perhaps you're in a season of life where your primary role is caring for someone, and time doesn't allow for much else? It can be hard to persevere when you feel an anointing, but it's attached to a 'not yet.'

Whatever we do with our time, our lives as Christians are a partnership, and your primary partner is the Holy Spirit. God knows where you are and why, and these prayers will invite Him to renew and equip you.

Your secondary partners are other Christians. These might be your church leaders, or faithful prayer warriors who've always got your back, praying into breakthrough. Perhaps you have mentors or accountability partners whom you trust to speak the truth in love? Praise God for them! There will be space to do that within these pages. You may also need to pray for provision of such people, if you aren't journeying with them currently.

When the whole body of Christ is working together, with Jesus Himself at the head, that's when we see the greatest blessing and growth. Praying for that is a great privilege and touches the Father's heart.

PRAYER 1

Reading: Ephesians 4:1-16

'Therefore I, a prisoner for serving the Lord, beg you to lead a life worthy of your calling, for you have been called by God.'
Ephesians 4:1

My............................,

Jesus, Your are no strange to opposition
    and neither was Paul.
Where I feel like a prisoner serving the Lord,
    I beg that You would supply me with all I need
    to live well, as You did.

I pray that I may live a life worthy of my calling,
    whatever that is.
Help me exhibit godly character,
    moral courage
    and personal integrity.
May my life radiate gratitude to You
    for my salvation,
    my calling
    and my partners in the gospel.
May I approach the work You've inspired
    with humility, gentleness
    and patience,
    leaning into Your timing in all things
    and leaning on Your word.

Journaling space

PRAYER 2

Reading: Ephesians 4:1-16

'Always be humble and gentle. Be patient with each other, making allowance for each other's faults because of your love.'
Ephesians 4:2

My Jesus,................................,

Thank You for your example in humility and service
        and in prioritising times of prayer
        alone with Your Father.
Please provide time for me to sit with You
and also prayer support for me;
        so that many are lifting me up as I seek to do Your will,
        and keeping me accountable.

Bless those who sit alongside me,
        in my workplace, my home and my church.
May they approach my works
        with the same humility and patience I desire,
        considering my efforts prayerfully.
Thank You for their wisdom.
May I accept it gracefully, for
        I want everything I do to be the best it can be
        for Your glory.

Thank You for those You've already given me
        to hold up my arms,
        as Aaron and Hur held up Moses

in the battle against the Amalekites.

Bless my supporters, mentors and partners abundantly
    and especially as I remember them now
    before Your throne of grace.
Keep us united in Your Spirit
    and bind us in the bond of peace.

My supporters are...

PRAYER 3

Reading: Ephesians 4:1-16

'However, he has given each one of us a special gift through the generosity of Christ.'

Ephesians 4:7

Abba Father,

Thank You for the gifts You have given me.
May I seek diligently to steward these gifts well,
    using them to build up Your body, the church.
Help me to be knowledgeable and helpful,
    but also kind, and
    overflowing with Your love.
Please provide me with mentors
    who will help me grow in my spiritual gifts
    and flourish in my calling.

Thank You for Your body, the church.
Give us all grace in proportion
    to Christ's rich and abundant gifts.
For when He ascended on high,
    He held captivity captive,
    and He bestowed Your Spirit upon us.
In our creation, You gave us talents,
    and through our rebirth, gifts of the Spirit.
Give me the grace to hold both well
    and put them to good use,
    not storing them up –
    as a man who buries his treasure in a field –
    but investing in the Kingdom of God.

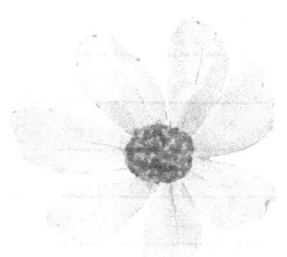

Journaling space

PRAYER 4

Reading: Ephesians 4:1-16

'Now these are the gifts Christ gave to the church: the apostles, the prophets, the evangelists, and the pastors and teachers. Their responsibility is to equip God's people to do his work and build up the church, the body of Christ.'

Ephesians 4:11-12

Jesus, my Messiah,
In Your church,
You have appointed some to be apostles,
      some prophets, some evangelists,
      some to guide and instruct.
For this purpose:
      To fully equip Your family – which includes me –
      for works of service,
      building up the body of Christ
      until we reach oneness
      in the faith and knowledge
      of the Son of God.
I can't wait for that day of glory!

Abba, bless me with good leaders
      and help me to sit well under them,
      learning from them and encouraging them.
May they be part of Your plan to equip me
      for what You have called me to.

Where I am a leader,
> fill me with Your Spirit,
> providing all I need to lead well,
> in humility and gentleness,
>> as I spur others on to godliness and maturity.

PRAYER 5

Reading: Ephesians 4:1-16

'Then we will no longer be immature like children. We won't be tossed and blown about by every wind of new teaching...'
Ephesians 4:14

My ....,

I ask You for discernment,
    so I may not be like an immature child,
    or a ship on a stormy sea,
    tossed back and forth on the wind.
Instead, be my anchor,
    helping me resist all shifting doctrine,
    deceitfulness and the devil's schemes.
May none of these things ever take root in my mind.
    Protect me, Jesus.
May none ever make their way into my speech,
    but keep it pure,
    sound
    and abundant with truth.
Regarding truth:
    May I always speak the truth with love,
    following the example of Jesus, my Messiah.
May my part of Your body work well,
    assisting the whole to grow and mature,
    as You build it up in unselfish, agapé love.

Amen.

Journaling space

SELAH

At the end of another busy week,

here's your chance to pause.

Be still in God's presence.

Let what you've prayed this week sink into your soul,

and let God speak.

What is He saying to you right now?

Journaling space

– WEEK 7 –

Reading: Ephesians 4:17-5:5

Having shown us the new abundant life we are called to, and spent some time thinking about our relationship with our new family, the church, Paul will soon expand on how to relate to those that belong to our 'old life' – those that might be more difficult to live with!

The introduction to this section is where we head next. It's summary? 'Imitate God' (5:1). Jesus is our example in godly living; He is the perfect embodiment of all the character traits God has – those that we are called to imitate in our dealings with others.

Paul takes us through several examples of what *not* to be, and they are all associated with darkness. It is difficult to read this passage (which runs into next week) without recalling John's incredible prologue to his gospel:

> The Word [Jesus] gave life to everything that was created,
>   and his life brought light to everyone.
> The light shines in the darkness,
>   and the darkness can never extinguish it.
> …The one who is the true light, who gives light to everyone,
> was coming into the world.
> …to all who believed him and accepted him, he gave the
> right to become children of God. They are reborn—not with
> a physical birth resulting from human passion or plan, but a
> birth that comes from God.
>   *John 1: 4-5, 9, 12-13*

As you dwell in these trickier final chapters of Ephesians, keep John 1 in mind, and remember that where you are called to go, Jesus has gone before you, lighting the way.

PRAYER 1

Reading: Ephesians 4:17–32

'Throw off your old sinful nature and your former way of life... let the Spirit renew your thoughts and attitudes. Put on your new nature, created to be like God—truly righteous and holy.'
Ephesians 4:22-24

My ....,
I put off my old self,
    completely discarding my former nature.
Instead, continually renew me
    by Your Holy Spirit speaking to my spirit.
Give me a fresh spiritual attitude and a new self
    created in Your image –
    blessed with righteous relationships,
    holiness and truth.

I reject all falsehood.
    and dwell not on anger.
I give the devil no opportunity to lead me into sin
    by continually repenting
    and refusing to cultivate bitterness.

Cultivate in me a spirit of generosity,
    for You held nothing back but
    gave Yourself freely for me.
Reveal to me areas where I might be stealing from others
    and combat my fear of radical generosity.

Journaling space

PRAYER 2

Reading: Ephesians 4:17–32

'*And do not bring sorrow to God's Holy Spirit by the way you live. Remember, he has identified you as his own, guaranteeing that you will be saved on the day of redemption.*'

Ephesians 4:30

My……………………………………,

Cleanse my heart so my words are wholesome:
      good for building others up,
      full of kindness and compassion,
      and a blessing to those who hear them.

Let me not grieve the Holy Spirit
      by any way that I live.
But keep my heart soft
      and open to your loving conviction.
You have identified me as Your own
      so help me to live accordingly.
Seal me, Holy Spirit,
      marking me for the day of redemption.
I want to live in constant communion with You
      knowing that my sin is not holding back
      any of Your precious blessing.

Help me to be kind to all,
      tenderhearted and forgiving.
Just as You, through Christ, have forgiven me.

Journaling space

PRAYER 3

Reading: Ephesians 5:1–5:5

'Imitate God, therefore, in everything you do, because you are his dear children.'

Ephesians 5:1

My............................,

I want to live a life pleasing to You,
    filled with love,
      imitating Your example.
You gave Yourself for me and so now,
    I give myself for You.

Infuse me, Jesus.
    So fill me that my every step is
    perfectly aligned to Yours,
    like a well-placed dance.
As You lead, may I follow
    with my hand gently placed in Yours,
    discerning each squeeze of your fingers,
    each subtle movement,
    and knowing exactly what they mean.
To follow Your lead is not to be dragged behind You
    but to be entirely in tune with You
    as Your Spirit dwells within me.

Journaling space

PRAYER 4

Reading: Ephesians 5:1–5:5

'Live a life filled with love, following the example of Christ. He loved us and offered himself as a sacrifice for us, a pleasing aroma to God.'

Ephesians 5:2

My Jesus, my Saviour,
Because You freely forgave me,
    may I imitate You by
    walking continually in love,
    practicing empathy and compassion,
    seeking the best for others as
    I look upon them with Your eyes,
    seeing their true needs and sacrificially serving.
You loved me.
You gave Your life for me.
But not just for me – also for them.
While it is true that
    I am Your beloved child,
        so are they.
May I see them as of such great value
    that You freely gave yourself up for them.
Yours was a sweet sacrifice;
    the most precious fragrance
    our senses could ever discern.
Thank You, Jesus.

Journaling space

PRAYER 5

Reading: Ephesians 5:1–5:5

'Obscene stories, foolish talk, and coarse jokes—these are not for you. Instead, let there be thankfulness to God.'
Ephesians 5:4

My..,

Your sacrifice was a pleasing aroma to God.
By contrast, our impurity reeks.
    It is a bloody stain upon Your name.
The lust for power, possessions and people – even hints of it –
    taint the church.
Let me not forget that my behaviour,
    my speech,
    my sly remarks and
    subtle hints
    all testify to the validity of my faith.
Forgive me for all filth,
    all evil that sits on my tongue like a bitter taste,
    especially after it has left my mouth.
Cleanse me and fill me instead
    with praise.
May thankfulness be on my lips,
    that my speech may reflect
    a heart wholly devoted to You;
    a heart in which no idolatry exists.
Where nothing is of greater value than my Jesus.
                                  Amen

Journaling space

SELAH

At the end of another busy week,

here's your chance to pause.

Be still in God's presence.

Let what you've prayed this week sink into your soul,

and let God speak.

What is He saying to you right now?

Journaling space

– Week 8 –

Reading: Ephesians 5:6-33

Now we move into the really tricky part of Ephesians – the bits that, for centuries, have been misused to justify oppression. If it has been read this way, it has been read wrong.

It is essential to keep these passages in the context of the entire letter, which is why the first two prayers focus on that. Paul is certainly not condoning submission to an abusive situation. Indeed, the entire letter up to this point has been about commencing a new, godly life of freedom in Christ, and imitating Him. Paul is speaking to a particular group of people in a specific cultural, historical space and time, applying principles from the first part of the letter to them in a practical manner. To transport his phrases mindlessly into a different context is unhelpful and damaging. Instead, we should seek to apply the earlier truth into our context, with the Holy Spirit's help.

Please don't skip these verses, like you would skip an embarrassingly messy bedroom when giving a friend a tour of your house. Everyone reading this will have different life experiences. No family is perfect, and none of us are either. If you are single or divorced, you may wish to adapt some of the prayers to fit your situation. Try to engage meaningfully with the principles behind the words, applying them to the relationships you do have, and remembering where we have journeyed thus far in the book.

I hope that by praying these sections of Scripture this way, they will bless you as much as the rest.

PRAYER 1

Reading: Ephesians 5:1-14

'For once you were full of darkness, but now you have light from the Lord. So live as people of light!'

Ephesians 5:8

My..,

You are truth, so protect me from deceit.
May I see Your truth, and not be won by
      empty arguments that ignite Your wrath.
I long to walk in the light of the Lord,
      giving no headspace for darkness
      but being a child of light,
      born again into Your blessed Kingdom.
Root me deeply into good soil.
Prune away all sickness and parasite behaviours.
Cut off any branches that are at odds with Your direction.
Produce in me the fruit of light –
      goodness,
      righteousness
      and sincerity,
      as I learn what is pleasing to You.
May I refuse to participate in shadowy deeds,
      instead, exposing them by living with integrity,
      even when that takes enormous courage,
      and by exhibiting godly character
      that flows from Your Spirit within me.

Journaling space

PRAYER 2

Reading: Ephesians 5:1-14

'...for the light makes everything visible. This is why it is said, "Awake, O sleeper, rise up from the dead, and Christ will give you light."'

Ephesians 5:8

My..,

All things become visible when exposed to the light
    of Your precepts.
So, may I not be ashamed.
May I walk with the light of Your countenance upon me,
    full of grace and freedom.
Awaken me now to this new life.
Where I am asleep, rouse me.
Call me from my slumber.

I renounce deaf ears,
    listening only to the voice of Jesus.
Awaken my dawn:
    A new life with honour,
    purpose, courage,
    wisdom and discernment.
I rise from the dead, for Christ will shine in me.
Give me boldness to take every opportunity
    to shine Your light
    into the lives of others.

Journaling space

PRAYER 3

Reading: Ephesians 5:15-33

'Don't be drunk with wine, because that will ruin your life. Instead, be filled with the Holy Spirit.'

Ephesians 5:18

My.................................,

These days are filled with evil,
    and it is easy to get bogged down.
It is easy to remain foolish;
    ignorant of the spiritual battle being waged.
But fill me with the Spirit
    and I shall have no need of the world's temptations.
Wine shall hold no power over me,
    for the Spirit's fullness is altogether more invigorating,
    fortifying, exciting,
    edifying, enlightening
    and pure.
I want You, Holy Spirit, more than any stimulant
    the world offers.
Be my passion and my guide.

Fill me with songs I may sing to my siblings in Christ,
    revelling in the joy of our salvation and
    the unity of our peace.
Giving thanks to you – God, our Father –
    Maker of all things,
    in the name of Jesus, our Saviour and brother.

Journaling space

PRAYER 4

Reading: Ephesians 5:15-33

'And further, submit to one another out of reverence for Christ.'
Ephesians 5:21

My..,

Out of reverence to You,
    may I consider others as better than myself.
Out of reverence to You, may I serve.

My spouse is the person You've given me to live closest with;
    I bring them before You now.
I ask that You would supply anything that is lacking
    in their faith,
    as I have prayed for myself.
I want them to know Your steadfast love and faithfulness
    as assuredly as I do.
May I serve them as You served me –
    with wholehearted devotion
    even when that costs me.
Where they exercise headship over me,
    may I bear it with grace,
    respecting their position as my protector
    and spiritual partner.
Where they are failing in this regard, Jesus help them.
    Sanctify them by Your Holy Spirit.
    Bring deliverance,
    revealing to them Your incredible work on the cross.

Journaling space

PRAYER 5

Reading: Ephesians 5:15-33

'For husbands, this means love your wives, just as Christ loved the church. He gave up his life for her to make her holy and clean, washed by the cleansing of God's word.'
Ephesians 5:25-26

Jesus, ……………………………………,

You are the Servant King –
    the one who came not to be served,
    but to serve,
    giving Your life as a ransom for me
    and my spouse.
May they seek to love me as You love me,
    surrounding me with caring, unselfish, sacrificial love.

Help me to do this also for them.
For You gave Yourself up for us,
    cleansing us by washing us with Your Word.
So You might present us as a bride
    in glorious splendour,
    without spot or blemish.
    Holy. Blameless. Set apart.
May I love my spouse as I love myself,
    nourishing, protecting and cherishing them
    as You nourish, protect and cherish Your church.
Keep my spouse and I faithfully devoted to one another
    and to You:

Seeking the best for one another
    with an attitude of lovingkindness.
Respecting and delighting in one another
    as we grow up into the body of Christ –
    treasured,
    honoured,
    and holding each other dear. *Amen*

SELAH

At the end of another busy week,

here's your chance to pause.

Be still in God's presence.

Let what you've prayed this week sink into your soul,

and let God speak.

What is He saying to you right now?

Journaling space

— Week 9 —

Reading: Ephesians 6:1-9

Continuing in this section of Ephesians, Paul addresses other relationships that dominate our everyday – our parents, our children and our colleagues.

Whether we had good parents or bad, the Bible constantly exhorts us to treat them with respect, and this doesn't end when we leave home. In an ideal situation, we'll learn from them and benefit from their wisdom, contributing to a good life. Yet, that ideal (which sadly, often doesn't happen) isn't what Paul highlights here. He highlights the promise – God's promise. When we do what is right, God is looking out for us. And He is trustworthy, even when our earthly parents fail.

Paul is radically countercultural by spending as much time addressing the parents as the children, and particularly, fathers. In a culture where fathers tended to be harsh and demanding, Paul points us back to God. Because we have a patient, loving, Heavenly Father, we have a good example for parenting (even if we didn't have a good earthly father).

Lastly, slavery. Remember the principle about keeping this passage in the context of the entire letter. Once again, Paul is certainly not condoning or supporting slavery. It was an everyday reality in his time, and he was teaching people – both slaves and masters – how to live well together in the (usually unavoidable) situation they were already in. There is so much here that we can apply to our own working relationships, and I hope that these prayers will help you to consider these scriptures in a new light, committing those relationships to your God.

PRAYER 1

Reading: Ephesians 6:1-9

'Fathers, do not provoke your children to anger by the way you treat them.'

Ephesians 6:4a

My ....,

Help me to honour those
    who have cared for me in the past,
    whether they did a good job or not.
Where they still hold authority over me,
    may I accept their guidance and discipline,
    that it may go well with me.
Even where I disagree,
    may I esteem those whom you've given me
    and seek the best for them.

You are the perfect Father.
May I learn from You,
    seeking to care for others as You care for me.
Help me not to provoke,
    being unreasonable,
    or exasperating with trivial demands.
May I never humiliate my children,
    nor show favouritism,
    but treasure them each as a precious gift.
I am their custodian here on earth,
    but You are their perfect, Heavenly Father.

Protect me from selfish indifference to their needs and desires.
May I raise them tenderly,
    with lovingkindness that flows from your Holy Spirit.

Those I'm praying for are...

PRAYER 2

Reading: Ephesians 6:1-9

'Rather, bring them up with the discipline and instruction that comes from the Lord.'

Ephesians 6:4b

My ....,
You are love,
    the perfect example;
    the source of all that is good.
Help me to live that example,
    not demanding from those in my care
    anything I cannot achieve myself.
In mercy and compassion,
    may I demonstrate Your grace,
    especially when I must discipline.
May my instruction in the Lord flow from a genuine,
    close walk with You,
    so I do not just impart head knowledge.
Instead, may they be convinced of Your truth
    by seeing Your love alive in me.
For Your love is patient and kind; not jealous,
    boastful, proud or rude.
Your love keeps no record of wrongs but freely forgives.
Your love doesn't rejoice in injustice but in truth.
It never gives up, never fails,
    but always remains hopeful and abundant in faith,
    enduring through every circumstance.
May Your love be my love, now and forever.

Journaling space

PRAYER 3

Reading: Ephesians 6:1-9

'Slaves, obey your earthly masters with deep respect and fear. Serve them sincerely as you would serve Christ.'

Ephesians 6:5

My ………………………………….,

Help me to live in right relationship with
    those dearest to me
    and those far away;
    those in authority over me,
    and those under my authority.
May I treat all as You would treat them.
For You are my Master in heaven,
    and You have no favourites.

Help me to respect those I work beneath.
When they do things that rile me inside,
    help me to act like Jesus,
    turning the other cheek,
    not legitimising what is wrong but
    being respectful and hardworking in all things.
You were led like a lamb to the slaughter.
On days when I feel this is my lot,
    help me to remain unblemished –
    a pure and spotless lamb who shows them Jesus.

Journaling space

PRAYER 4

Reading: Ephesians 6:1-9

'Try to please them all the time, not just when they are watching you. As slaves of Christ, do the will of God with all your heart.'

Ephesians 6:6

My ....,
You have the most beautiful heart,
    a heart pure and lovely.
Please give me a sincere heart
    that I may work as well when my boss is watching
    as I do when they are not watching.
For You are my true Master
    and You never do wrong.
You are my true Master
    and every sacrifice made is made unto You.

You see all things, and yet, You love.
Help me to do Your will from my heart,
    working for them as if I am working for You,
    knowing that my reward is in glory.
I strive, therefore, for the crown of life;
    the victors crown that shall be mine
    when I have completed this race.
Thank You that You have gone before me,
    enduring all things for my sake.

Journaling space

PRAYER 5

Reading: Ephesians 6:1-9

'Masters, treat your slaves in the same way. Don't threaten them; remember, you both have the same Master in heaven, and he has no favorites.'

Ephesians 6:9

My ....,

Thank You that I sit under Your authority,
      having You – the perfect judge – as my example.
I praise You that I am fearfully and wonderfully made;
      in Your image, I have access to Your justice.
Where I have authority over others,
      may I show them constant goodwill,
      requiring nothing that will cause them to stumble,
      respecting their time and their value
      as a child of God.
When my tongue has practiced wrong,
      cleanse it,
      and give me the courage to ask for forgiveness.
May gossip and slander never pass my lips
      but may I have,
      and be known for having,
      perfect integrity.
For You are our true Master and there is no partiality
      with You,
      between me or them.

Amen

Journaling space

SELAH

At the end of another busy week,

here's your chance to pause.

Be still in God's presence.

Let what you've prayed this week sink into your soul,

and let God speak.

What is He saying to you right now?

Journaling space

– Week 10 –

Reading: Ephesians 6:10-24

We're nearing the end of a ten-week journey through this incredible letter. For the past few weeks, we've considered the difference between walking in the old way and the new way, particularly as regards our relationships with others. Paul doesn't doubt this will be hard!

When we follow the way of Jesus, we will face opposition, not just from those around us, but also from our enemies in the spiritual realms. Remember what Paul wrote earlier?

> God's purpose in all this was to use the church to display his wisdom in its rich variety to all the unseen rulers and authorities in the heavenly places (Eph. 3:10).

For

> [God] raised Christ from the dead and seated him in the place of honor at God's right hand in the heavenly realms. Now he is far above any ruler or authority or power or leader or anything else... (Eph. 1:20-21).

Christ has been placed above every other spiritual power – and the devil doesn't like it!

Therefore, we need the armour of God. We need it for every aspect of our lives, but particularly when we're doing things that glorify Jesus' name. When we're bringing Jesus glory, we will find ourselves in spiritual battles.

This is how we fight our battles – with prayer! The battle can be subtle – discouragement is one of the enemy's most powerful weapons – but it can also be fierce. When you feel like you're surrounded, come back to this week and fight that battle, knowing that after the battle, you will still be standing firm. Take courage, my friend!

PRAYER 1

Reading: Ephesians 6:10-24

'A final word: Be strong in the Lord and in his mighty power.'
Ephesians 6:10

To the only God my Saviour,
    Rich in mercy and abundant in faithfulness,

I long to be strong in You.
Draw me to Yourself,
    empowering me through our union,
    in the authority of Your boundless might.
I put on the full armour of God
    that I may successfully stand
    against all the strategies and schemes of the devil,
    who seeks to steal my faith
    and prevent me from fulfilling my calling.
I know this is a spiritual battle.
    He will attack
    when I'm releasing something that honours You
    and builds Your kingdom.
He doesn't want that to reach the world.

Therefore, I put on Your full armour,
    that I may successfully stand:
    Fully prepared,
    Immovable
    And victorious.

Journaling space

PRAYER 2

Reading: Ephesians 6:10-24

'Stand your ground, putting on the belt of truth and the body armor of God's righteousness. For shoes, put on the peace that comes from the Good News so that you will be fully prepared. In addition to all of these, hold up the shield of faith to stop the fiery arrows of the devil.'

Ephesians 6:14-16

My ....,
I put on Your full armour,
      the body armour of Your righteousness
      won for me by Jesus,
      who was without sin.
I tighten the wide band of truth around my waist
      leaning on the promises You've given me,
      On your holy word,
      abundant in stories of your faithfulness.

I strap to my feet the gospel of peace,
      knowing this is my message and my salvation.
      A story of reconciliation won
      and reconciliation to come.
I lift up the protective shield of faith
      which You've gifted me with and built up within me.
      With it, I can extinguish every flaming arrow.
They shall not sink in,
      but disintegrate before they reach me.

Journaling space

PRAYER 3

Reading: Ephesians 6:10-24

'Put on salvation as your helmet, and take the sword of the Spirit, which is the word of God.'

Ephesians 6:17

Wonderful Saviour, Yeshua,

I take the helmet of salvation,
    pushing it firmly on my head.
There it guards my mind from all the devil's lies,
    all his accusations,
    all his claims that I am not good enough.
For You are good enough – and You have won my sure place
    in Your kingdom.

These lies shall not take my mind captive,
    for I know whom I have believed.
It is not by my works
    but by the blood of Christ that I am saved.
Recall to my remembrance all the truths You have taught me;
    truths from Your Word.
Saturate my soul with them until there is no room for lies,
    and falsehood simply bounces off my helmet.

Where I am not in good habits, help me.
I know that I need this helmet
    and I need Your Word.
Provide opportunities for drinking more deeply
    of Your living water,
    and may I never pass them up for lesser things.

Journaling space

PRAYER 4

Reading: Ephesians 6:10-24

'Pray in the Spirit at all times and on every occasion. Stay alert and be persistent in your prayers for all believers everywhere.'
Ephesians 6:18

My ………………………………….,

Thank You for the Sword of the Spirit
    which I take up now.
That double edged sword
    pierces the hardest hearts.
This sword is Your Word,
    illuminated to the softened heart,
    penetrating soul and psyche.
May my words be a sword too,
    sharpened for those
    You have chosen to hear them.
Oh, Holy Spirit, prepare hearts to receive Your truth
    by my tongue.

So, I pray.
I pray at all times, in every season.
I pray in the Spirit, allowing Him to speak more than me.

Keep me alert,
    watchful, prayerful, persistent.
    And in tune with Your voice.
Keep my armour strong and effective.

Journaling space

PRAYER 5

Reading: Ephesians 6:10-24

'And pray for me, too. Ask God to give me the right words so I can boldly explain God's mysterious plan that the Good News is for Jews and Gentiles alike.'

Ephesians 6:19

My…………………………………..,

Thank You for bringing people into my life
    to share the Good News with me.
I remember them now,
    and praise You for them.

For others whom You have called to share
    the good news of Your kingdom:
I pray that words may be given to them,
    that when they open their mouths,
    their notebooks or their screens,
    words may flow,
    proclaiming boldly the mystery of good news.
Give us all courage and boldness.
May we be for each other as Tychicus was for the Ephesians:
    A comfort,
    Encouragement
    And strengthener of hearts.
May peace and grace abide
    in all who love my Lord Jesus
    with an undying and incorruptible love. *Amen.*

Those who shared with me…

Those whom I share with…

SELAH

At the end of this prayer book,

here's your chance to pause.

Be still in God's presence.

Let what you've prayed this week sink into your soul,

and let God speak.

What is He saying to you right now?

Journaling space

FINALLY,

'Peace be with you, dear brothers and sisters, and may God the Father and the Lord Jesus Christ give you love with faithfulness. May God's grace be eternally upon all who love our Lord Jesus Christ.'

Ephesians 6:23-24

ABOUT THE AUTHOR

Natasha Woodcraft lives in a slightly crumbling farmhouse in Lincolnshire with her husband, four sons and a menagerie of animals.

She holds an honours degree in Theology and believes stories have power to communicate deep truth and transform lives. Her novels explore God's redemptive purposes for ordinary, messy people living in biblical times. Also a songwriter, Natasha peppers her emotional prose with poetry and song.

She's part of the team at Broad Place Publishing, a UK publishing house specialising in Christian fiction, and is a founding member of the Kingdom Story Writers.

ALSO BY THE AUTHOR

The Wanderer Series

"You shall be a fugitive and a wanderer on the earth."

1. The Wanderer Scorned
Cain & Abel reimagined

2. The Wanderer Reborn
Can hope triumph after the first murder?

2.1. The Wanderer's Sister
*A Novelette exclusively for the author's reader club.
Sign up at:*
https://natashawoodcraft.com/subscribe

ABOUT THE PUBLISHER

Broad Place Publishing is an independent publisher, passionate about bringing to market quality books that Jesus wants the world to read. We look for creative ways to support our authors and distribute our books as widely as possible.

https://broadplacepublishing.co.uk

www.ingramcontent.com/pod-product-compliance
Lightning Source LLC
Chambersburg PA
CBHW072056110526
44590CB00018B/3195